DRIVE THRU
DECEPTION

CLUES TO
DETECT
DECEIT

LAURIE AYERS

RICHARD
Reese

Drive-Thru Deception by Laurie Ayers

RICHARD Reese
7702 Harold Avenue
Jenison, MI 49428

Substantive Editor: Kent R. Jones
Proofreader: Elizabeth Wiegner
Interior Designer: MartinPublishingServices.com

Publisher: RICHARD Reese

RICHARD
Reese

ISBN: 978-0-9996041-0-6 (print), 978-0-9996041-1-3 (epub)

1. Self Help 2. Business 3. Reference

First Edition

Printed in the United States of America

If this book whets your appetite for more,
visit www.LaurieAyers.com

CONTENTS

HAVE YOUR CAKE & EAT IT TOO / 119

MORE ABOUT THIS LIE LADY, LAURIE AYERS / 132

APPETIZERS

If Actions Speak Louder Than Words, Then Why is the Pen Mightier Than the Sword?

Actions speak louder than words, right? Put your money where your mouth is. Walk the talk. Those are wildly accepted principles.

However, when it comes to deception detection, words always speak louder than actions.

Drive-Thru Deception shows you a method to detect deception. This method is sometimes referred to as content analysis or forensic statement analysis. It uses words instead of actions, and it is the most accurate and reliable way to determine if someone is lying.

This proven method entails paying close attention to the actual words someone writes or speaks. Unlike body language, content analysis requires no interpretation, and you can determine credibility without the need to see the person making the statements.

People lie for many reasons, but they can be broadly summed up by two motives:

1. To avoid punishment or a painful situation or

2. To get a reward or something they desire.

Everything a person says has meaning. Ask yourself: *Why did he say it that way?*

Keep reading for more bite-size clues to deceit. Each chapter is a quick read and set up to stand alone. Take each nugget and put it into practice immediately.

To Read Without Reflecting
is like Eating Without Digesting

When it comes to deception detection, words always speak

_____ .

People lie for many reasons, but they can be broadly summed up by two motives:

1.

2.

EVERYTHING
A PERSON
SAYS HAS
MEANING.

A Slip of the Tongue, and Not In a Good Way

Most people love to talk. Some never seem to shut up. You've heard the phrase "Give them enough rope to hang themselves"? In lie detecting, that is exactly what you want to happen. The more they say, the more words you have to find the consistencies and the discrepancies. Even those who say they don't want to talk can still give you enough words to work with.

People mean exactly what they say, therefore you can use their words to uncover deception; they just don't always intend to say what comes out of their mouth or fingers. If you use the information I share in this book, you will pick up on what they did not mean to slip out. Many times, the slip of the tongue will be extremely subtle.

You can use this process to detect deception whether you're reading a statement, email, or letter, or if you're listening to them speak in person, on the phone, or digitally.

Most deceptive stories will not be completely false. It's important to remember that a lie is an attempt to deceive. Omission is the most common method of deception. Therefore, it'll be your job to find out what information is missing.

To Read Without Reflecting is like Eating Without Digesting

Most deceptive stories will not be

_____ .

_____

is the most common method of deception.

"

NO ONE
BELIEVES A LIAR.
EVEN WHEN
SHE'S TELLING
THE TRUTH.

SARA SHEPARD,
HEARTLESS

Anything That Costs You Peace of Mind is Too Expensive

I assume you are reading this book because you have some interest in getting better at knowing when you're being deceived. Although, deception detection isn't so much about catching someone in a lie, it's more about your ability to have more peace of mind in making sound decisions.

A January 26, 2015 article in Forbes headlined, "Workplace Stress Responsible For Up To $190B In Annual U.S. Healthcare Costs." I've seen other studies that claim this amount is as high as $300 billion. Regardless of what dollar amount you assign to stress, we know that it can certainly take a toll on our mental and physical well-being.

How could learning to detect deception give you peace of mind? For starters, you could have more confidence and serenity about the actions you take and choices you make.

For example, if you're responsible for new hires, would it help you to be able to discern if candidates are being truthful during the interview?

As a litigator, would it bring you peace of mind to have the ability to instantly recognize, with confidence, when the person testifying isn't telling you the whole story?

Or perhaps you suspect your significant other is cheating on you. Would it give you peace of mind if you had a way to tell if you're being paranoid or have valid concerns?

Learning to uncover deception using a person's own statements can give you peace of mind to recognize when something is amiss. There are certain words and phrases that indicate someone is attempting to deceive you. You will learn that something as seemingly insignificant as an article (the vs. a) can signal deception.

To Read Without Reflecting
is like Eating Without Digesting

Deception detection isn't so much about

_____ ,

it's more about your ability to

_____ .

66

NO MAN HAS A
GOOD ENOUGH
MEMORY TO BE A
SUCCESSFUL LIAR.

ABRAHAM LINCOLN

More Confidence Than a Naked Toddler Wearing a T-shirt on His Head

Learning deception detection through words can give you confidence to probe further to find out more. Does this situation sound familiar? You suspect someone is lying, so you question them. But you're told that you're crazy, paranoid, or out of your mind. You're led to doubt your suspicions.

Once you know which words and phrases can signal deceit, you'll be able to stand your ground and dig deeper to uncover deception, or confirm the truth. You'll be able to proceed with more confidence than a naked toddler wearing a t-shirt on his head.

Peace of mind, confidence, and contentment— that sounds pretty good to me.

To Read Without Reflecting
is like Eating Without Digesting

Once you know which _____ and _____ can signal deceit, you'll be able to stand your ground and dig deeper to uncover deception, or confirm the truth.

If It Walks Like a Duck,
and Talks Like a Duck...

If it walks like a duck, and talks like a duck, you're probably drunk, because ducks don't talk. Circumstantial evidence is not evidence. Absence of evidence is not evidence.

Believing a lie can be equally as damaging as disbelieving the truth. Accusing someone of lying without having ground truth can irreparably damage a relationship.

Unless you have ground truth—not what appears to be evidence, but actual, solid proof—it'd be irresponsible to state someone is absolutely lying. Ground truth is hard evidence or direct observation. It's not a sense or an inference.

Forensic statement analysis can help you pinpoint specific areas that need deeper consideration or more probing. The results of your acute follow-up may lead you to ground truth, or to a confession.

To Read Without Reflecting
is like Eating Without Digesting

Believing a lie can be equally as damaging

as _____.

Ground truth is _____ or

_____ .

I Miss You, Captain Obvious

If you only focus on catching someone in a lie, you may miss the truth. People will say, "I know he's lying," when they really mean it appears there is a lie. What they know is that something seems off or that the words aren't matching up.

You may be confident someone is withholding or skewing information; or it may be obvious they are uncomfortable. Those are keen observations, but those behaviors do not automatically mean someone is lying.

Often, I ask, "How do you know for certain they are lying?" I sometimes get responses such as: I just do. Because he wasn't where he said he was. Because she's a liar. Because I know her/him. You'd have to be an idiot not to know that's a lie.

Those are responses from people who are determined to catch someone lying. Odds are, some of those people they knew were lying, were indeed not being truthful. Yet I can say with a high certainty, some of them were probably telling the truth, but the biases didn't allow it to be seen.

Not everything that doesn't add up is a lie; but it may be something they don't want you do know, so they word it strangely in attempt to mislead you. Think how much better your relationships would be if, in the absence of ground truth, you focused on looking to verify the truth instead of concluding it to be a lie.

To Read Without Reflecting
is like Eating Without Digesting

If you only focus on

_____ ,

you may miss the truth.

Think how much better your relationships
would be if, in the absence of ground truth,
you focused

_____ .

"

NOT EVERYTHING
THAT DOESN'T
ADD UP IS A LIE.

I Wasn't Lying; You Didn't Ask the Right Questions

There's a scene in the HBO TV Show, True Detectives, when Matthew McConaughey's character is being questioned and is told, "I figured you'd be the one to know." He responds, "*Then start asking the right f-ing questions.*"

Avoid asking compound questions. If you ask, "Were you really at work and had an emergency meeting?" she could answer, "Yes I really was." However, you don't know what she's answering yes to. She may have been at work, but not working.

Ask one question at a time. Then wait for an answer. Don't interrupt. Deception can be uncovered in their words—so let them give you words.

If there's too much silence, and you absolutely feel you need to say something, then respond with "I'm listening..." or "Go on." Ask open ended questions. Remember, you want to keep them talking.

Ideally, instead of asking a question that ends in a question mark, (Why is she texting you?) use a sentence that ends with a period (Tell me about …). Using this technique should get a lengthy response because you asked a broad question (broad meaning expansive, not broad as in floozy). If you get a very brief answer, your storyteller is being deceptive and withholding information.

Be very careful not to give them the answer. "You weren't really going to change the figures, were you?" The way the question is worded begs for a "no" response. Instead, ask "Did you change the figures?" Better yet, you will get more information if you say, "Tell me about how the figures got changed."

To Read Without Reflecting
is like Eating Without Digesting

Ask one question at a time. Then

_____.

Instead of asking a question that ends in a
question mark, use a sentence that

_____.

2

COULD YOU
REPEAT THAT
PLEASE

Pete and Repeat Were In the Boat. Pete Fell Out, So Who Was Left?

When you start to hear repetition it's an indication they are thinking about what to say next. This shows their story is not coming from memory, but rather being made up. If they repeat your question, e.g., "Did I work late?" and there's no obvious reason to believe your question was not heard properly, they're stalling for time and it's an indication that you've struck a nerve.

Also listen for emphasis, "Did **I** work late?" "Did I **work** late?" "Did I work **late**?" They may be planning on fancy word play or for a starring role in the Bob & Weave show.

Further, if they mention the same portion of the story more than once, the same conclusion can be drawn, that they're stalling for time to make something up or that you've struck a nerve.

When he testified during the Senate Intelligence Committee hearing on June 8, 2017, former FBI Director, James Comey was asked about his meetings with the president.

"Guess I don't know for sure. I believe the — I take the president at his word, that I was fired because of the Russia investigation. Something about the way I was conducting it, the president felt, created pressure on him that he wanted to relieve. Again, I didn't know that at the time, but I watched his interview, I've read the press accounts of his conversations. So, I take him at his word there. Now, look, I — I could be wrong. Maybe he's saying something that's not true. But I take him at his word, at least based on what I know now."

To Read Without Reflecting
is like Eating Without Digesting

---

is an indication they are thinking about what to say next.

"

THREE THINGS
CANNOT BE
LONG HIDDEN:
THE SUN, THE MOON,
AND THE TRUTH.

BUDDHA

Children Never Misquote; They Repeat Exactly What You Shouldn't Have Said, Word for Word

Usually copying a statement verbatim is viewed as plagiarism. However, in deception detection interviews it is vital that you repeat exactly what someone says. In truthful statements, the vocabulary shouldn't change.

For example, if the story is about a guy, it should remain consistent about "a guy". If you refer to him as "a man" instead of a guy, then it's possible the storyteller could switch his vocabulary. If you are the reason for the change, it will taint your ability to accurately evaluate credibility because you've suggested the change to him. Whereas if he changed on his own from referring to a guy as a man, that is key and could indicate an untruthful statement.

Listen for changes. Normally, when someone starts with one word, they continue with it. (The bar vs. the pub, car vs. vehicle, shoes vs. boots). If they suddenly change, investigate further, because there may be more going on than what you're being told.

Use the same words they use. If they call it a meeting, you call it a meeting. If they say sleep with, you say sleep with. There are no synonyms in forensic statement analysis.

This is important because their exact words can be very telling, especially if they say something that seems out of place.

LAURIE AYERS

To Read Without Reflecting
is like Eating Without Digesting

In truthful statements, the vocabulary

_____ .

There are no _____
in forensic statement analysis.

66

PEOPLE WILL
BELIEVE A BIG LIE
SOONER THAN
A LITTLE ONE.
AND IF YOU REPEAT IT
FREQUENTLY ENOUGH,
PEOPLE WILL
SOONER THAN
LATER BELIEVE IT.

WALTER LANGER

You Say Potayto;
I Say Potahto

Don't confuse your personal dictionary with theirs. A common word that means different things to different people is "hurt". Some view the word hurt to only mean physical pain. Then there's the issue of what degree of pain. Some may not view a bruise or small scrape as being hurt. Others may decide anything that causes any kind of pain is being hurt. What about being emotionally hurt or financially hurt?

In this digital age, the word "contact" can also mean different things to different people. "I haven't had any contact with her" may mean no physical contact. Or it may mean no voice-to-voice communication. Or it may mean no communication at all, no text, no email, no Facebook, nothing. The takeaway here is not to interject your own definition of words. Ask the person to elaborate or give you their personal definition of a word.

To Read Without Reflecting
is like Eating Without Digesting

Do not _____

your own definition of words.

I Can Neither Confirm Nor Deny

Unless someone says they did not do the specific thing they're being accused of, it's not a real denial.

Sometimes it only sounds like a denial. They may deny the conclusion (I'm not guilty), but they won't deny the act (I didn't delete the files).

A truthful person will answer specific questions with direct responses, whereas a deceptive person avoids answering the question.

Because people don't want to outwardly lie, guilty people will often do a word dance to make you think they are denying it without actually saying they did not do it. Some phrases they may use instead of a true denial include:

- I couldn't do that
- I wouldn't do that
- I could never do that
- I had nothing to do with

- I am innocent
- I am not guilty
- There is no evidence
- I deny doing that
- I haven't done anything

They want you to believe it is impossible for them to have done what you're suggesting. They want you to conclude they haven't done it.

When these phrases are used, you cannot believe they did not do it, because they have not told you they have not done it. When people give a denial, look to see if they denied specifically what they are accused of or if they merely denied the conclusion that others believe they are guilty.

In 2008, Casey Anthony was charged with the murder of her daughter. She was found not guilty in 2011. Here is an excerpt from a March 7, 2017 interview she gave to the Associated Press, underlines added to highlight this point.

"She talks of [now] working on a DUI manslaughter case [as an assistant to her former case investigator] where the accused took a plea deal. *'I look at him and I think this kid almost lost his life for something <u>they can't definitively prove that he did</u>,' she said. 'I've lived it firsthand. <u>I didn't do what I was accused of</u>."*

To Read Without Reflecting
is like Eating Without Digesting

They may deny the _____,
but they won't deny the _____.

Name three phrases they may use instead
of a true denial:

1.

2.

3.

That's What She Said

Phrases such as "If I had to say" or "I would say" are similar to the disingenuous denials we just covered. They are used to avoid telling an outward lie, and to make it appear they are saying something they aren't.

After an Oakland County, Michigan court hearing on October 9, 2017, pediatrician Dr. Daniel Schnaar, addressed the issue of whether or not some vaccinations contained aborted fetal DNA. He responded, "If I had to testify, I would say that vaccines are not made from aborted fetuses."

Note: The CDC website lists vaccine ingredients taken from the manufacturers' package inserts. As of this writing it shows that there are currently over two dozen vaccines that are developed using aborted fetal cell lines and contain human DNA. They are listed by their cell lines such as WI-38, MRC-5 or as human diploid cells.

https://www.cdc.gov/vaccines/ubs/pinkbook/downloads/appendices/B/excipient-table-2.pdf

To Read Without Reflecting
is like Eating Without Digesting

Phrases such as "If I had to say" or "I would say" are used to

_____ ,

and to make it appear they are

_____ .

3

SECRET
MENU
ITEMS

You Can't Un-see It

There are certain words and phrases people use to try to beef up their statement, in an attempt to convince you they are being truthful. After you learn what they are, you'll forever listen to and read statements differently. Once you see it, you can't un-see it.

What many liars don't know is that by using these words, it usually backfires on them. Instead of boosting their credibility, it actually weakens their statement.

Here is a partial list of deception markers often used.

- *Trying.* "I'm trying to be honest." Trying means attempted but failed.
- "I'm being as honest as possible." *As possible* doesn't mean completely.

- *For sure.* "I can't say for sure." Can't say? Or won't say? For sure? Meaning there is something you know about it.
- *At all.* "I don't know what's going on at all." See *For sure*.
- *Really.* "I don't really talk to her anymore." Not really, maybe just a little.
- *Actually.* "Actually, I received a call." If it's not comparing two things, such as if no one asked if they received a text or if they're still waiting on a response, then the use of the word actually signifies deception.
- *Could, couldn't, would, wouldn't.* "I would never do that." These words do not mean that they <u>didn't</u> do that.
- *Never.* "I would never do that." If asked, "Did you do [that]?", it's a yes or no question. Never doesn't mean no.
- *I am not capable* of that.
- *Possibly, Maybe.*
- *In fact. I'm certain.*
- *I swear to God. Honestly, to tell the truth, honestly, frankly, truthfully.* When people say truthfully, it usually isn't.

To Read Without Reflecting
is like Eating Without Digesting

List five words and phrases people use to try to beef up their statements & bolster credibility:

1.

2.

3.

4.

5.

"

NEVER
DOESN'T
MEAN NO.

I Have No Idea

"I have no idea" or "I don't have a clue" are deceptive responses. Everyone has at least *some* thought or indication what may have happened. To say they have "no idea" is a way of withholding information.

If someone responds with this, let them know that you're not suggesting they *know* what happened. You want to know what they *think* may have happened. Ask them to take a wild guess what may have happened. Their response may be an indirect way of telling you what they did.

Another tactic is to ask them what they think should happen to anyone who did that. If they say something harsh, like "Prosecute to the fullest extent of the law," "Hang the SOB by his junk in a public place," or "Take him for every penny," you're likely dealing with someone who did not do what he is accused of, and truly wants the one who did it brought to justice.

However, if the punishment seems mild for the accused such as, "It was probably a misunderstanding," "Sounds like there is a mental health issue that needs addressing," or "Everyone makes mistakes," then it's a strong likelihood the person you're speaking with did do it.

LAURIE AYERS

To Read Without Reflecting
is like Eating Without Digesting

When someone responds to question-
ing about what they think happened with
"I have no idea," ask them what they
think should happen to anyone who did
that. If they respond harshly, it indicates
_____. Whereas if
the consequences seem mild, it is a strong
likelihood that

_____

_____

_____.

"

ONE LIE
HAS THE POWER
TO TARNISH A
THOUSAND TRUTHS.

AL DAVID

I'm Just Checking to Make Sure You're Okay

The word "just" is often used to minimize things. When the word just is used, it almost always means there is something else going on. "I just wanted to…" "I just thought …" "I was just talking to him about the game."

During a September 2016 interview with Dr. Phil, Jon-Benet Ramsey's brother, Burke, was asked what he did after his mom frantically entered his room screaming Jon-Benet was missing. Burke replied, *"I just laid there. I didn't really know what else to do."*

Burke wanted us to believe all he did that morning was lie in bed after his mom came in his room hysterically looking for his sister. He used the word just to minimize his actions, and it indicates he may have done some other things besides stay in bed while there was chaos around him. Because he knows other actions transpired, it caused him to unknowingly use the word just.

Then Dr. Phil mentioned how it seemed odd he'd just lie in bed. Burke responded. *"I don't know, I guess I just ... felt safer there?"* This doesn't necessarily indicate he is lying, but it does signify other things happened that he is not saying.

To Read Without Reflecting
is like Eating Without Digesting

The word "just" is often used to

_____ .

Use of the word "just" doesn't necessarily indicate someone is lying, but it does signify _____ .

**WHO LIES
FOR YOU
WILL LIE
AGAINST YOU.**

BOSNIAN PROVERB

I Only Had Three Beers, Ociffer

Some people say that 666 is the devil's number. Or that when you see 11:11 on a clock, someone is thinking of you. In deception detection, the number three (3) is a liar's number.

When you hear or see the number three, pay attention. It's the number most often used in deceptive statements. "I only had three beers." "I texted her three times." "When I walked out of the mall, three guys were standing by a van." "I had $30 in my locker." "I left work around three o'clock." "We just hung out and watched *13 Going on 30*, on Netflix."

Former FBI Director, James Comey testified during the Senate Intelligence Committee hearing on June 8, 2017. When he was asked about his meetings with President Obama he said, *"And I — I — as I said in my written testimony, as FBI director, I interacted with President Obama. I spoke only twice in three years and didn't* document it." "In fact, I just remembered, sitting here, a third one [interaction]. When — you've seen the picture of me walking across the Blue Room." "The next Friday, I have dinner, and the president begins by wanting to talk about my job. And so, I'm sitting there, thinking, "Wait a minute, three times, we've already — you've already asked me to stay, or talked about me staying."

To Read Without Reflecting is like Eating Without Digesting

When you hear or see the number _____, pay attention as it is considered a liar's number and most often used in deceptive statements.

"

WE PAY A
PERSON THE
COMPLIMENT OF
ACKNOWLEDGING
HIS SUPERIORITY
WHENEVER WE
LIE TO THEM.

SAMUEL BUTLER

I Am 100% Certain
That I Am 0% Confident
In What I Am Saying

When someone uses the word "certain" or "confident" it indicates they are thinking about other possibilities. After careful consideration, they then conclude they are convinced [this] is what happened or will happen. If a person is certain or confident of something, they won't use the word "certain" or "confident." Someone who has done nothing wrong probably would not contemplate being found guilty.

In November 2016, the FBI announced it was reopening the email investigation on Hillary Clinton, as it was reported 650,000 new emails were discovered. In her press conference regarding this new revelation, Clinton said, *"I'm confident, whatever they are [new emails], will not change the conclusion reached in July."* A more credible sentence would have been, "The new emails will not change the conclusion reached in July." Even better, would have been a statement that addressed the alleged wrong-doing, not the conclusion.

Also from the Casey Anthony March 7, 2017 AP interview: "Discussing Caylee's last moments, the 30-year-old Anthony spoke in halting, sober tones: *'I'm still not even certain as I stand here today about what happened,'* she said."

To Read Without Reflecting
is like Eating Without Digesting

When someone uses the word _____ or _____ it indicates they are thinking about other possibilities.

Someone _____ probably would not contemplate being found guilty.

"

PERHAPS WE HAVE
BEEN GUILTY
OF SOME
TERMINOLOGICAL
INEXACTITUDES.

WINSTON CHURCHILL

Don't Get Me Started

When someone says something was "started," it means the act was interrupted or never completed. "He started putting his hand up my skirt." A truthful statement would be, "He put his hand up my skirt." If the act was interrupted or never completed, listen for the rest of the statement that tells why it was interrupted.

In the case of a reported assault, if someone is saying he started to do something, it's reasonable to then hear the alleged victim say something like "I told him to stop," or "I pushed him off," or "I was so scared all I could do was…" If there is nothing describing the interruption, it's likely an untruthful statement, and there is a good chance she is making up the story.

Sexual assault must be taken very seriously, but so should false claims. Unfortunately, we've recently seen some women claim "me too" to get their 15 minutes of fame.

Falsely accusing someone only hurts the real victims and can ruin someone's life if they did not do what they're accused of.

What do you make of this actual account told to the media?

"After the dinner was cleared he began encroaching on my side of the seat. [He] started coming over to me and groping me and trying to embrace me. And then his hands started going up my skirt."

To Read Without Reflecting
is like Eating Without Digesting

When someone says something was "started," it means the act was _____ or
_____.   When this happens lis-
ten for the rest of the statement that tells
_____. If there isn't
more to the statement, it likely did not
happen.

"

WHEN TRUTH
IS REPLACED
BY SILENCE,
THE SILENCE
IS A LIE.

YEVGENY YEVTUSHENKO

Do I Look Familiar to You?

Next up is Articles. I hope I'm not giving you English class flashbacks. These refreshers will come in handy in your quest for the truth. Articles are words that define a noun as specific or unspecific. Articles determine ownership vs. distance, and familiarity vs. stranger.

For example, if I said, "A man walked up to me." That sounds like it's a stranger, or random man, right? Whereas if I said, "The man walked up to me." Then we can assume he's someone I've seen or mentioned before. There has already been some familiarity with the specific man we're talking about.

The same goes for This and That, These and Those. This guy vs. that guy. "This" and "These" are specific, definitive, close and familiar. "That" and "Those" are distant and stranger.

This is important because if someone is trying to convince you of something random, unknown or unspecific, but uses articles that indicate familiarity, then there is deception occurring.

To Read Without Reflecting is like Eating Without Digesting

Articles determine ownership vs. distance, and _____ vs. _____.

"This" and "These" are _____, _____, _____ and _____. "That" and "Those" are distant and stranger.

"

I'M NOT UPSET
THAT YOU LIED TO ME,
I'M UPSET THAT
FROM NOW ON
I CAN'T BELIEVE YOU.

FRIEDRICH NIETZSCHE

What's the Meaning of This? Oh, It's a Pronoun

The use of pronouns does not necessarily indicate deception. However, when names are missing it is something to notice as it can signal deception by trying to distance themselves from what they are saying happened. It can also indicate they're not terribly fond of the person. "The" wife is not nearly as endearing as "my" wife, or better yet, using her actual name.

If someone doesn't want to be attached to the tale they are spinning, the pronouns may be missing. In the documentary "Vaxxed," Bill Gates makes the following statement:

"Well, Dr. Wakefield, ah, has been shown to use absolutely fraudulent data. Created a fake paper. The journal allowed it to run. All the other studies were done, showed no connection whatsoever…"

He failed to say He created a fake paper [referring to Wakefield]. Gates also did not say they showed no connection... [referring to all the other studies].

Note: This is the same paper that many inaccurately refer to as "a study that said vaccines cause autism." When in actuality, this was not a study, but rather a minor paper, and nowhere in the paper does it state any such causation. Rather it concluded that they "did not prove an association between the MMR and the syndrome described," however there was the possible predisposition should be looked into further.

In additional to omitting pronouns, deceptive people may also try to over compensate by using "I" too many times. I did this. I did that. I ... I ... I ....

Using the word "you" instead of "I" is another red flag.

Deceptive: "What happened on that cruise in Greece is not something that you want to think about. You bury it. It's not something you want to remember, but you also can't forget."

Truthful: "What happened on that cruise is not something that I want to think about. I keep it buried. It's not something I want to remember, but I also can never entirely forget."

We, us, they, I, me, mine, our, his, hers, yours, and theirs can be deceptive if they're used instead of, not in addition to, names.

Changing pronouns in the same story is also an indication of deception. "I went into *my* office" shows accepting possession and closeness of his office. Then if later in the story you hear he "went back to *the* office," the change from "my" to "the" shows he no longer wants to be associated with his office and is trying to distance himself from it.

To Read Without Reflecting
is like Eating Without Digesting

The use of pronouns does not necessarily indicate _____. However, when names are missing it is something to notice as it can signal deception by trying to

_____ .

Using the word "_____" instead of "I" is another red flag.

Oui We Monsieur

"We" is a plural pronoun. It indicates more than one person is involved. However, if you hear "we" but no one else has been identified, there either wasn't more than one person, or the identities of those involved are being intentionally left out. This is also true for "us." If no names are mentioned they are concealing the identity of those involved or there is not a good relationship between them.

Both "we" and "us" indicate some kind of partnership or dual responsibility. If you heard "we did this or that" but it involves a heinous situation, such as a mugging, attack, kidnap or rape, then it is a deceptive story. There should be no partnership between the victim and the perpetrators of a crime.

To Read Without Reflecting
is like Eating Without Digesting

Both "we" and "us" indicate some kind of
_____ or _____. If you heard
"we did this or that" but it involves a heinous situation, such as a mugging, attack,
kidnap or rape, then it is

_____ .

4

HOURS OF OPERATION

And the Next Thing I Knew It Was Thursday

Most people leave out some details when they recount a story. Thankfully they do; it's painful to have to sit through every single, nitty gritty detail of a story. However, more than just for the sake of brevity, deceptive people intentionally omit significant details.

Identify gaps in time. This is where the omitted details are likely to be. Words and phrases that are commonly inserted to skip over those areas they do not want to talk about include: *The next thing I knew, the next thing I remember, after, after a while, later, or later on.*

If you want to get more verification that they're either fabricating or omitting, ask them to repeat their chain of events in reverse chronological orders. Most who are deceptive will attempt to memorize their story, but won't bother to practice it backwards.

In April 2017, Gary Giordano was found liable for the wrongful death of traveling companion Robyn Gardener during their trip to Aruba in 2011. Here is part of his testimony.

"… then she came out of the water. It looked like she had lifted her toe on the rocks. So, she laid down. Then at some point it looked like she fell asleep a little bit so I let her have her peace. After a little while she woke and I said, "Hey, do you want to go back hotel? Or jump in and take a look at the fish?"

To Read Without Reflecting is like Eating Without Digesting

---

is where omitted details are likely to be.

List two words or phrases that are commonly inserted to skip over those areas they do not want to talk about:

1.

2.

"

A HALF-TRUTH
IS A WHOLE LIE.

YIDDISH PROVERB

If Your Watch is Broken, You're Going to Have a Bad Time

When reading a statement or listening to an account of past events, are the time references consistent? Or does it flip flop between specifics, "at 230," then change to approximations, "around four"? Are there big chunks of time missing? "Left work at 5, got to the gym at 7, got home around 930"; yet you know it doesn't take 2 hours to get from work to the gym and they are members of a gym that only has 30-minute workouts.

Many of you may remember watching parts of the Casey Anthony trial in 2011 when she was facing charges in the death of her daughter. She testified that she took her daughter to the nanny between 9:00am and 1:00pm. That's a mighty big window of time.

Lastly, if time references are out of order, it's another deception marker. "I got to work at 0800, went to lunch at 1300, got to the library at 2000, and left work at 1700."

To Read Without Reflecting
is like Eating Without Digesting

When reading a statement or listening to an account of past events, are the time references _____ and in _____?

Her Pants Were Set on Fire

Remember learning about passive vs. active voice in school? No, probably not, so here is a quick refresher: I set her pants on fire (active). Her pants were set on fire (passive). Children who don't want to be punished often use a passive voice, "The lamp fell over." Adults are also guilty of using the passive voice, "The phone died." "The gun went off." (passive) instead of "I didn't plug my phone in or have a charger." "I had a negligent discharge." (active).

When someone uses passive language, they are trying to avoid responsibility and omit the names of those involved. They don't want to say I did this or I didn't do that, especially if it's a lie, so it's easier to make a passive statement.

To Read Without Reflecting
is like Eating Without Digesting

When someone uses passive language, they are trying to avoid _____ and omit the _____ of those involved.

The Past, the Present, and Future Walked Into a Bar. It Was Tense.

Verb tenses refer to the time the action is taking place. When someone retells what they saw or what happened, they should be speaking in past tense because it already happened and is coming from memory.

Using the present tense to retell what happened in the past indicates the statement is being made up. "So, we're walking into the store and this guy approaches." A more truthful statement would be "As we walked into the store, a guy approached."

If you want to see another example of using present tense when recalling a past memory, flip back a few sections to **I Only Had Three Beers, Ociffer.** You can reread FBI Director Comey's statement about meeting with POTUS.

Lastly, you sometimes hear past tense used when a loved one speaks out about a missing person,

"She was a beautiful girl," but supposedly she's still alive—unless they know that not to be the case. "She is a beautiful girl" would be a better statement for a missing case.

To Read Without Reflecting is like Eating Without Digesting

Using the present tense to retell what happened in the past indicates

_____

_____ .

"

IF YOU TELL
THE TRUTH,
YOU DON'T
HAVE TO
REMEMBER
ANYTHING.

MARK TWAIN

"I Asked Her to Marry Me and She Said, 'Yup.' The End."

Deceptive stories end quickly. There is a scene in the movie, The Proposal, when Sandra Bullock and Ryan Reynold's characters (Margaret and Andrew) were telling the engagement story to the family. If you saw the movie you also know that it was a deceptive story.

The set-up and all the details leading up to the actual proposal were extensive and elaborate. Then Andrew jumped in and said, *"I asked her to marry me and she said 'Yup.' The end."* He was quick to get off the story.

One clue to deception is how well the statement is balanced. A truthful statement about what happened has a beginning, during, and after ratio of approximately 25%, 50%, 25%. It is in balance.

A deceptive story will be off balance or unevenly weighted. If someone is not being truthful about what took place, the beginning, during, and after ratio will be closer to 35%, 50% 15%. It will have more lead-in to set it up and then a quicker ending to get off that subject.

Clearly there's a little wiggle room in those percentages. The key is that it should be balanced with the beginning and ending of similar length. If the statement tends to end abruptly, there's a strong possibility deception is involved.

To Read Without Reflecting is like Eating Without Digesting

Deceptive stories end _____.

A truthful statement about what happened has a beginning, during, and after ratio of approximately _____, _____, _____.

5

EMOTIONAL
EATING

I Was So Afraid I Couldn't Move

In a truthful statement, felt emotion will come after an incident is over. If you've ever hit a deer with your car, you know that it happens so quickly that while the incident is in progress you're not thinking about how scared you are. After it's all over and you realize what just happened, then you may be shaking, upset, startled, or scared.

In a deceptive story, there may not be any emotion shared in the details, or the storyteller will insert it in the wrong place—typically in the beginning or middle of the incident because that's where they think it should go.

To Read Without Reflecting is like Eating Without Digesting

In a truthful statement, _____ will come after an incident is over.

In a deceptive story, there may not be any

_____, or the storyteller will insert it in the wrong place.

Punctuation is Everything. Is it "A woman, without her man, is nothing" or "A woman: without her, man is nothing"?

If a written sentence doesn't have any punctuation at the end, pay attention. This is generally an indication the person has more information that she is not willing to share. Their complete thought has not been finished.

OMG!!! I have to tell you about exclamation points. Most people, if they exclaim in writing, use only one exclamation point. If there is an instance when multiple exclamation points are used, then that is generally to show high emotion or excitement. The key here is to look for consistency. If in the statement, there is one, one, one, then three exclamations points and the words don't match up with something that would normally warrant three, that's a sign it's deceptive. The text was either written by someone else, or it's not a true emotion.

I am a prime example of this one. I rarely use exclamation points, and when I do, it's always only one. People who know me, know that if they ever see anything with more than one exclamation point, they can be assured, I did not author it.

To Read Without Reflecting is like Eating Without Digesting

In written statements look for _____ in the punctuation and that it matches up with _____.

"

RESORTING TO
LYING OR CHEATING
IN ANY COMPETITION
AMOUNTS TO
CONCEDING DEFEAT.

GEORGE HAMMOND

You're Acting Inappropriate to My Inappropriate Behavior

Are the verbs appropriate and as you would expect them to be? For example, if someone was retelling a story about being attacked but she said, "He [the alleged attacker] SAID, "Don't look at me." Would it be appropriate to use the verb "said"? Or if the attack really happened, would he have more likely "yelled," "demanded," or even "told" her not to look at him. "Said" is an inappropriate verb to describe what supposedly was taking place.

In August 2016, Olympic Swimmer Ryan Lochte told his mom that he and his buddies were robbed at gun point in Rio. It didn't take long for Ryan to admit that he lied. Before coming clean, he gave an interview detailing what happened. *"We got pulled over, in the taxi, and these guys came out with a badge, a police badge, no lights, no nothing just a police badge and they pulled us over."*

Look at the verbs he used to describe getting robbed at gunpoint, "We got pulled over … and these guys came out." Ryan is American.

In the U.S., "getting pulled over" is generally a term used for a traffic stop. Getting pulled over is not typically something that is rushed or violent. When the police want to pull someone over, often they will flash their lights and the driver just knows they better pull over. Instead of the suspects "rushing the vehicle or storming it," he told us they "came out." For someone whose primary language is English, "pulled over" and "came out" are not generally used to describe a crime in progress.

Inappropriate verb usage is an indicator the statement is being made up.

This is a good place to mention that these content analysis clues to deceit are most applicable to someone with English as their primary language.

If someone is not a native English speaker, it may explain some of the discrepancies. Therefore that is vital information to have before you start any analysis or flag any words or phrases as deceptive.

To Read Without Reflecting
is like Eating Without Digesting

Inappropriate verb usage is an indicator the statement is _____.

If someone is _____, it may explain some of the discrepancies.

Sometimes !#%@ Is the Only Word to Describe The Situation

In genuine emotions, you are likely to hear harsh words because the true feelings are coming out. "That jackass had the nerve to…"

I've been known to spew some colorful expletives if idiot drivers are encroaching near me when I'm behind the wheel. *Yet another reason I don't talk with clients on the phone while I'm driving.*

If someone found out a trusted coworker or friend betrayed him, you would expect to hear some lively language. Whereas, a deceptive person either truly likes the person he is attempting to talk trash about, or simply has no ill feelings, so you're not likely to hear off-color remarks to describe the person. Occasionally, if someone is lying they will go overboard in trying to convince you how upset they are by using an excessive amount of cussing. This should be obvious to you as well.

To Read Without Reflecting
is like Eating Without Digesting

In genuine emotions, you are likely to hear
_____ because the
_____ are coming out.

6

I'D LIKE
TO ORDER

Which Came First?
The Chicken or the Egg?

Usually we tend to mention our kids in order they were born. If Bella was born first and Ruby second, you would not expect to hear Ruby and Bella. If you knew Patrice before she got married, you'd likely refer to the couple as Patrice and Chris. Yet if you knew Chris first, you'd probably refer to them as Chris and Patrice. Pay attention to the order which people and things are mentioned.

One of the best examples I could find to highlight the importance of paying attention to the order things are mentioned is taken from the infamous OJ Simpson "Suicide Letter." You can find this note with a simple online search.

He spoke of his relationship to Nicole Brown Simpson, saying that their marriage "had some downs and ups." The common phrase is "ups and downs," but because OJ reversed the order, this means there were more downs than ups in their marriage.

If an order is reversed from the norm, it does not mean the person is necessarily lying, but it is definitely something that should catch your attention. It's a good point to probe further about why something was mentioned out of order.

To Read Without Reflecting
is like Eating Without Digesting

Pay attention to _____ which people and things are mentioned.

It's a good point to probe further about why something was mentioned _____.

66

WHEN WITNESSES
CONCOCT LIES,
THEY OFTEN
MISS THE OBVIOUS.

JOHN GRISHAM,
THE TESTAMENT

You're Out of Order! You're Out of Order! The Whole Trial is Out of Order! They're Out of Order!

Here is something else to consider as it relates to the order in which a list of events or items is mentioned. Remember, when we're retelling from memory, we shouldn't have too much trouble listing the order as it happened or as it belongs. Though if making it up, there's no memory to rely upon, so the story could be out of order. Sometimes the out-of-order list isn't terribly obvious. "We went to a party at 921 Knapp St. in Grand Rapids, MI, apartment number 3." Most people would give the apartment number before the City and State. Mentioning it at the end indicates distancing. This person doesn't want to be associated with the apartment. You will want to find out why this is the case.

Keep reading to learn about how the placement of words in a sentence means something.

To Read Without Reflecting
is like Eating Without Digesting

If someone is making up a story, there's no
_____, so the story could be out
of order.

What is an example of distancing?

_____

_____

_____

Your Earlobes Are the Same Distance Apart as Your Nipples

Look where people are situated in relation to the other people in a statement. The word "with" is considered distancing language.

Saying "My girlfriend and I went to the Earth, Wind and Fire concert" is not the same as saying "I went to the EWF concert with my girlfriend."

"My girlfriend and I" is joining two people together. "I went with my girlfriend" means he didn't really want to go. *Although I personally can't imagine any reason, someone wouldn't want to hear EWF groove that night in September. Who knows, maybe it was after the love was gone.*

An easy way to remember this point is by looking at the distance between the people in the sentence. It is easier to tell a lie using the word with, than using the word and.

Keep in mind that the word with means distance; it does not mean deception. However, this is still important to note because generally if someone is being deceptive they will try to distance themselves from the person or situation. We saw this in the previous example where the apartment number was listed after the City, State.

To Read Without Reflecting
is like Eating Without Digesting

The word "with" means _____;
it does not mean deception. But it is
important to note because it indicates
_____.

7

HAVE
YOUR CAKE
AND EAT IT
TOO

Your Nose Is In the Middle of Your Face Because It's the Scenter

Most know the story of Pinocchio as the wooden boy whose nose grew every time he told a lie. But did you know that he only lied once? That was when he told the Blue Fairy that he did not go to school because he and Jiminy were captured by monsters. That one lie has given him the reputation of a liar.

In deception detection, there is no Pinocchio's nose. Can you imagine how fun politics and the nightly news would be if there were such a thing?

There is not one single indicator that will alert you if someone is lying. Your determination about one's credibility should not be made simply because they used a lone word or phrase commonly associated with deceit. Nor should a timeline that doesn't add up be used to determine someone is lying.

We haven't talked about baseline yet. If you know someone frequently uses one of the words or phrases mentioned in this book, that does not necessarily mean the person frequently lies. I know someone who often says, "To be honest with you." We know that is a liar's phrase. However, for this person, it's merely part of her vocabulary. When someone's personal way of speaking *changes*, when there is a change from baseline, that is noteworthy.

You must consider several factors or clues to deceit before resolving the status of their truthfulness.

LAURIE AYERS

To Read Without Reflecting
is like Eating Without Digesting

Explain what is meant by "There is no Pinocchio's nose."

_____

_____

_____

_____

"

PEOPLE NEVER LIE
SO MUCH AS
AFTER A HUNT,
DURING A WAR,
OR BEFORE AN
ELECTION.

OTTO VON BISMARCK

Practice Safe Texts

You've just about finished *Drive-Thru Deception*, what's next?

Now that you have some knowledge of how to tell if someone is lying using words, you need to build the skillset. In order to do that, you need to practice. Once you get good, you'll pick up the clues to deceit mentioned in this book in real time, as you're hearing or reading them for the first time.

If you want to do an analysis, you should plan to invest some time digging into a transcript or watching and re-watching a video so that you can isolate all the inconsistencies, or verify the credibility.

Watching interviews on news programs such as Dateline, 48 Hours, 20/20, your local news or YouTube is a good way to practice your deception detection skills. Prepared speeches are not good examples to use. You want as much free-flowing, unscripted, unrehearsed content as possible.

I also like to do word search puzzles to keep my mind sharp and focused on finding words quickly. These are transferrable skills when analyzing written content in deception detection.

When I do an analysis, such as you can find on www.LaurieAyers.com, I often transcribe verbatim from a video interview. Then I begin to look at each word and mark up the paper like a middle school English teacher with a fresh red pen. I use underlines, circles, boxes and brackets to highlight words, phrases and omissions that are clues to deceit. It can be time consuming, but the results are inescapable and quite revealing.

To become masterful at this, and to be able to detect deception on the fly, it requires the ability to stay focused (Squirrel!) and to be a good listener. It's also imperative that you practice, and then practice some more.

To Read Without Reflecting
is like Eating Without Digesting

Name two ways to practice your new deception detection skills.

_____

_____

_____

_____

_____

_____

66

THE LAW REQUIRES
A PAPER TOWEL AD
TO BE SCRUPULOUSLY
HONEST, BUT
ALLOWS POLITICAL
CANDIDATES
TO LIE WITHOUT
REPROACH.

JEF I. RICHARDS

Pick Your Nose, Your Friends, and Your Battles

I've just given you the abbreviated version of deception detection using words to uncover deceit. I encourage you to use this information with caution, especially as you are trying out your new skills. Disbelieving the truth can be as damaging to relationships as believing lies.

If you're focused on finding a lie, you could miss the truth. Keep their entire statement in context, and consider the whole picture.

Everyone lies, some more than others. If you start calling everyone out on their half-truths, or even blatant lies, you could find yourself a very unpopular and lonely person.

Pick your battles. Decide if your acknowledging perceived deceit is worth the resulting potential damage to the relationship.

To Read Without Reflecting is like Eating Without Digesting

_____ can be as damaging to relationships as believing lies.

If you're focused on finding a lie, you

_____ .

Yes Please,
May I Have Another?

Now that you've had a taste of these bite-size clues to deceit, are you hungry for more? Be sure to visit www.LaurieAyers.com to learn more about how I can add value to your company, conferences and meetings.

If you enjoyed *Drive-Thru Deception*, the best compliment you can give is a referral. Thank you for telling your colleagues and friends about this book and my services. A brief review on Amazon.com is also appreciated; thank you.

#DriveThruDeception

To Read Without Reflecting
is like Eating Without Digesting

Where can you find more information about this subject or about having Laurie speak to your group?

_____

_____

What should you do if you enjoyed *Drive-Thru Deception*?

_____

_____

More about this Lie Lady, Laurie Ayers

Can you imagine what it would be like to have a spouse or girlfriend who has made a career out of detecting deception? It would take a very confident, and honest, person to be comfortable in that relationship.

Some think I am a mind reader, and they start confessing all sorts of things to me. I recall one such time during a week-long course I was teaching on credibility. Before the morning session started I was exchanging pleasantries with the delegates. I asked one if he had a nice evening or if he had an opportunity to explore the city. He hastily blurted out, "I DIDN'T DO THE REQUIRED READING!" I do have a keen ability to focus and listen intently, but I assure you, I cannot read minds.

I'm often asked how I got into the deception business. I'd like to clarify it's the deception *detection* business. I'm not a professional liar.

My journey into deception detection first began in the 1980s after I trusted the wrong guy with my safety. I continued my lie spotting training after I learned that monogamy didn't exist in my relationship (even though I thought it did). Finally, after watching the 5 o'clock news in 2009, I learned that my long-time friend and associate was being charged as a principal in a Ponzi scheme, the same person with whom I invested my retirement and daughters' college savings accounts with. It was at that moment I decided I was going to fully immerse and dedicate myself to becoming a deception expert.

I had always been considered intelligent and very good at research. I did not jump into any of the above without extensive and careful consideration. How could I have missed such high-stakes deception?

I was impassioned to make sure I learned everything factual about deception based on proven' scientific methods. I made it my mission to master the knowledge, skills and abilities in deception detection in order to share this valuable information with others so they could avoid similar painful experiences.

For years I've worked as a deception expert consulting in the corporate world with medical, law enforcement, litigators, news media and human resources professionals. This is a worthwhile and interesting niche to share my expertise. I'll work with anyone who wants to get to the truth, although these professions listed above tend to be the clients who seek out my services.

These same skills are transferable on a personal level as well. Parents want help to tell if their kids are lying, as well as peace of mind toward facility providers caring for their elderly parents. I regularly receive questions from people in relationships or wanting to get into a relationship so that they are able to feel more confident in their judgments with a significant other.

Today I'm the managing director of Concealed Statements where I get to consult with others about truth, credibility and deception. I love what I do. My business is so rewarding. If my prior experiences and my current expertise can help others from getting hurt, cheated on or scammed, then my day was not wasted.

As an author, analyst, and speaker I've helped people from all around the globe learn how to have the confidence and peace of mind that comes from believing the truth and disbelieving lies.

If you're interested in my full bio, including my credentials that set me apart from other forensic statement analysts you can learn more at www. LaurieAyers.com.

INDEX

Made in the USA
Middletown, DE
22 December 2019